For Those Who Grieve

Comfort and peace in times of sorrow

Dennis Jernigan

Photography by David Johnson

God understands your grief

because He, too, once lost

Someone He *loved*.

*Surely He has borne our griefs
and carried our sorrows.*
Isaiah 53:4

Pretending

that you don't hurt brings

temporary relief,

but like an *untended wound*,

a heartache ignored continues to fester.

The Lord is near to those
who have a broken heart.
Psalm 34:18

He knows

how to

God is an emotional God,

and you are created in His image.

get you through

the emotional realities

of life and loss.

So God created man in His own image; in the image of God He created him; male and female He created them.
Genesis 1:27

Don't avoid your emotions;

they are healing and cleansing agents

that can be used to your advantage

when placed in God's hands.

*From the end of the earth
I will cry to You, when my
heart is overwhelmed.*
Psalm 61:2

When you don't understand *why*,

trust

the One

than yours.

are higher

whose thoughts

LIMITED
SIGHT
DISTANCE

As the heavens are higher
than the earth, so are My ways
higher than your ways, and My
thoughts than your thoughts.
Isaiah 55:9

Stuffing all
the hurts you
feel can be
quite easy.

Not healthy,

but easy.

As for me, I will call upon God, and the Lord shall save me. Evening and morning and at noon I will pray, and cry aloud, and He shall hear my voice.
Psalm 55:16–17

share your sorrows

with Someone big enough

is being able to

to handle them

The joy of love

when you cannot.

God is our refuge and strength,
a very present help in trouble.
Psalm 46:1

Guilt

Someone

best carried by

is a burden

bigger

than *you.*

*Come to Me, all you who
labor and are heavy laden,
and I will give you rest.*
Matthew 11:28

Grief

is best walked through

when shared

with *another*.

A friend loves at all times.
Proverbs 17:17

Trust God

to be in control

even when you feel

out of control.

Trust in the Lord with all your heart,
and lean not on your own understanding;
In all your ways acknowledge Him, and
He shall direct your paths.

Proverbs 3:5–6

In the dark times of life,

it is sometimes easier

to see

the light of

God's love and presence

For You will light my lamp;
The Lord my God will
enlighten my darkness.
Psalm 18:28

It's OK
to withdraw
for a time.

Even Jesus

needed to get away

from the things

that drained Him of life.

*So He Himself often withdrew
into the wilderness and prayed.
Luke 5:16*

It's OK to fall

apart in

Jesus' arms.

When

you cannot

hold

yourself together,

God can.

Be merciful to me, O God,
be merciful to me! For my
soul trusts in You; and in
the shadow of Your wings
I will make my refuge.
Psalm 57:1

In a quiet place,

it's sometimes easier to hear

God's still, small voice.

I will hear what God the Lord will speak, for He will speak peace to His people and to His saints.
Psalm 85:8

Grief is best endured

when you cease trying to play God—

when you cease

your

striving

and simply seek

to know Him more

intimately.

When you said, "Seek My
face," my heart said to You,
"Your face, Lord, I will seek."
Psalm 27:8

When you can't pray,

you have One with the power to

transform

even your tears of weakness

into prayers for help...

and those prayers do not fall upon deaf ears.

The Spirit also helps our weaknesses. For we do not know what we should pray for as we ought, but the Spirit Himself makes intercession for us with groanings which cannot be uttered.
Romans 8:26

You don't have to

thank God

for the bad things—

just for

being there

in the midst of them.

For I am persuaded that neither death
nor life, nor angels nor principalities
nor powers, nor things present nor
things to come, nor height nor depth,
nor any other created thing, shall be

many more times

than you

have given Him

credit for,

and He

will redeem

you   *again*.

*Through the Lord's mercies we are
not consumed, because His compas-
sions fail not. They are new every
morning; great is Your faithfulness.*
Lamentations 3:22–23

Give yourself permission   to   *move*   on:

God does.

Forgetting those things which are behind and reaching forward to those things which are ahead, I press toward the goal for the prize of the upward call of God in Christ Jesus.
Philippians 3:13–14

surprises

God sends little

to remind you

to keep on

loving and living.

*In the multitude of my anxieties within
me, Your comforts delight my soul.*
Psalm 94:19

Which is the greater hurt:

to love and be wounded

or to die never having known the joy *of sharing life with another?*

I will turn their mourning
to joy, will comfort them,
and make them rejoice
rather than sorrow.
Jeremiah 31:13

Hold memories as

treasures

in your heart

until the day

you can hold your loved one

in God's presence.

I thank my God upon every
remembrance of you.
Philippians 1:3

Memories are treasures

that earthly wear and tear

cannot corrupt or corrode,

and thieves cannot

steal or destroy.

Lay up for yourselves treasures in heaven...where thieves do not break in and steal. For where your treasure is, there will your heart be also.
Matthew 6:20–21

Jesus loved,

risked His life,

suffered loss.

Yet from His loving,

for life.

came our hope

His risking,

His loss,

Blessed be the God and Father of our Lord Jesus Christ, who according to His abundant mercy has begotten us again to a living hope through the resurrection of Jesus Christ from the dead.
1 Peter 1:3

How would you know

the refreshing power of the rain

if you never knew

the searing dryness of the drought?

I knew you in the wilderness,
in the land of great drought.
Hosea 13:5

Unconditional love

is

a gift

that pain and suffering cannot negate

and death cannot sever.

*For the mountains shall depart and the
hills be removed, but My kindness shall
not depart from you. Nor shall My
covenant of peace be removed.*
Isaiah 54:10

Life,

with all its sorrow,

can be a joyful journey

that culminates in eternal life,

where death and sorrow,

suffering and tears

will be no more.

And God will wipe away every tear from their eyes; there shall be no more death, nor sorrow, nor crying. There shall be no more pain, for the former things have passed away.
Revelation 21:4

From Dennis Jernigan

The words found in this book were born out of my own journeys through grief and were forged in the flames of loss. Many of the lives that inspired these words are now living on a higher plane, having left this world to take their place in another—with God.

My prayer is that you would find hope and comfort for your soul wherever you are in the journey and that you would remember that you are never alone. Learn to rest in the comforting arms of the Lord and listen for that still, small voice. In His arms you will find what you are looking for.

Dennis Jernigan is an award-winning recording artist who has released twenty-one albums and published three previous books: *A Mystery of Majesty*, *This Is My Destiny*, and *Help Me to Remember*. Dennis, his wife Melinda, and their nine children live in Oklahoma.

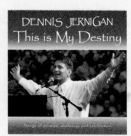

We Will Worship
CD/Cassette

I Surrender
CD/Cassette

Songs of Ministry
CD/Cassette

This Is My Destiny
CD/Cassette

**Like Christmas All
Year 'Round**
CD/Cassette

Available Where Christian Products Are Sold!

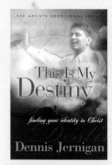
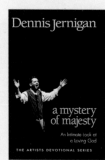

This Is My Destiny
Devotional Book

**A Mystery of
Majesty**
Devotional Book

Our purpose at Howard Publishing is to:

- *Increase faith* in the hearts of growing Christians
- *Inspire holiness* in the lives of believers
- *Instill hope* in the hearts of struggling people everywhere

Because He's coming again!

For Those Who Grieve © 2002 Dennis Jernigan
All rights reserved. Printed in China
Published by Howard Publishing Co., Inc.
3117 North 7th Street, West Monroe, Louisiana 71291-2227

02 03 04 05 06 07 08 09 10 11   · 10 9 8 7 6 5 4 3 2 1

Project editor, Philis Boultinghouse
Concept and design by Mike Rapp, Gear, Nashville, Tennessee
Photography by David Johnson, Nashville, Tennessee
Author photograph by Matthew Barnes, Nashville, Tennessee

Library of Congress Cataloging-in-Publication Data
Jernigan, Dennis.
    For those who grieve : comfort and peace in times of sorrow /
    Dennis Jernigan.
        p. cm.
  ISBN 1-58229-217-5
    1. Consolation. 2. Bereavement—Prayer-books and devotions—English. I.
Title.

BV4905.3 .J475 2002
248.8'66—dc21
                                                    2001051478

Scripture quotations are taken from The Holy Bible, New King James Version,
©1982 by Thomas Nelson, Inc.